This Book Belongs To:

_____

Color Test Page

Positive thinking makes it happen

The best bridge between despair and hope is a good night's sleep.

E. Joseph Cossman

WHEN THE flower blooms, the bees COME UNINVITED.

- Ramakrishna

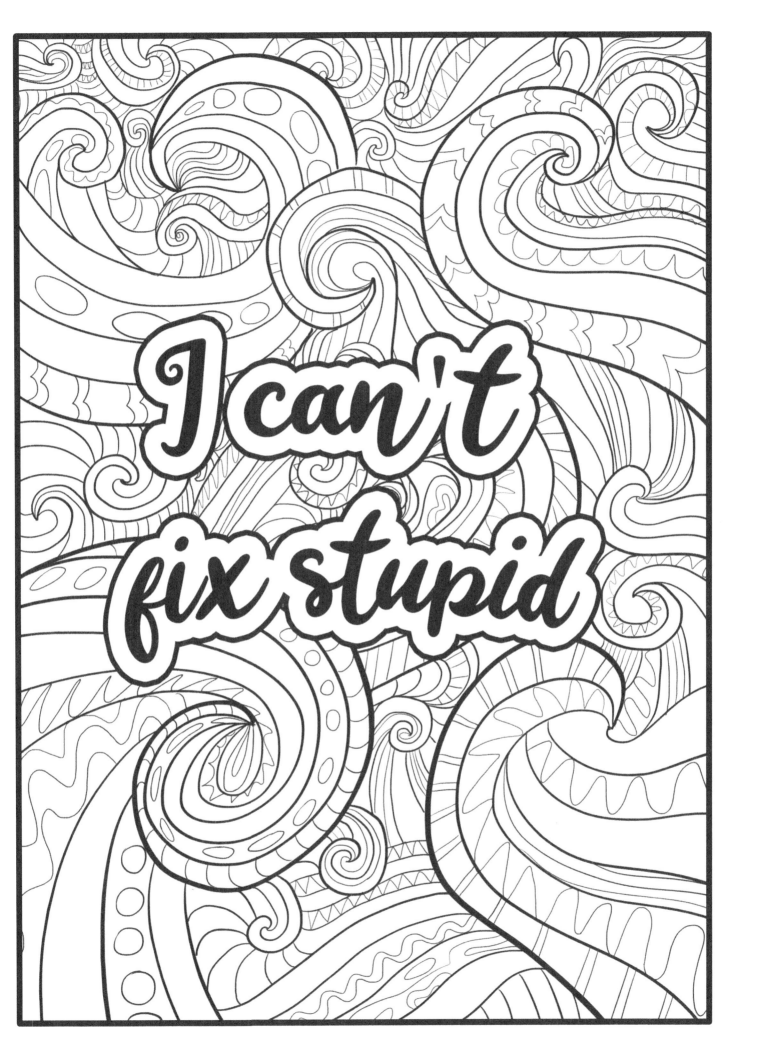

As the sun shines both on the cedar tree and the smallest flower, so the Divine sun illumines each soul.

Therese of Lisieux

Made in the USA
Las Vegas, NV
05 May 2024

89494164R00031